What Was the Industrial Revolution?

by Jim Gigliotti

illustrated by David Malan

Penguin Workshop

For Barb and Eric, the most
industrious people I know—JG

For my builders Emmett and Calvin—DM

PENGUIN WORKSHOP
An imprint of Penguin Random House LLC
1745 Broadway, New York, NY 10019
penguinrandomhouse.com

Library of Congress Cataloging-in-Publication Data is available.

First published in the United States of America by Penguin Workshop, 2025

Manufactured in the United States of America
CJKW

ISBN 9780593754252 (paperback)
10 9 8 7 6 5 4 3 2 1

ISBN 9780593754269 (library binding)
10 9 8 7 6 5 4 3 2 1

The authorized representative in the EU for product safety and compliance
is Penguin Random House Ireland, Morrison Chambers, 32 Nassau Street,
Dublin D02 YH68, Ireland, https://eu-contact.penguin.ie.

Contents

What Was the Industrial Revolution?

One day in 1830, two groups of train passengers gathered in Baltimore, Maryland, to witness an unusual race.

One group climbed into a train car on the Baltimore and Ohio Railroad rail line. On a track right next to it, several people climbed into another car. Those train cars were not at all like they are today. Train cars in the early nineteenth century

were not enclosed spaces with comfortable seats and nice windows to look out of. They were more like wagons. They often moved coal from place to place. And they were pulled by horses!

That's what made this race so different. The first train car was to be pulled by a horse, as usual. But the second train car—well, this was something new. It was to be pulled by a machine: a steam locomotive. The locomotive was designed and built by the American inventor Peter Cooper. It was fueled by coal.

Cooper's machine was not very big. It was only thirteen feet long and weighed about ten thousand pounds. Compare that to a modern locomotive, which often is about seventy-six feet long and weighs more than four hundred thousand pounds. Cooper's machine was so small that it soon was nicknamed the Tom Thumb, after the boy in a seventeenth-century fairy tale who was the size of a thumb.

The two tracks on the Baltimore and Ohio

line were side by side for about thirteen miles to Ellicott's Mills, Maryland. That's how far the race would be. The horse started off at a trot and took the lead. But Cooper furiously fed the furnace of the Tom Thumb shovelfuls of coal, and the machine picked up speed. (The coal burned to create steam, which powered the engine.) The Tom Thumb passed the horse and soon was moving at almost fifteen miles per hour. No horse could keep up with that while pulling a train car filled with people.

It looked like the Tom Thumb was sure to win. The locomotive pulled farther and farther away from the horse-drawn train. Suddenly a belt on the Tom Thumb broke loose from a pulley! The locomotive slowed to a stop. The horse trotted past.

Because of the mechanical trouble, the horse won the race that day in Maryland. Still, it was obvious that it was just a matter of time until steam-powered locomotives took the place of horses.

Indeed, when this race took place, the age of machines had already begun. This was a time known as the Industrial Revolution, the period when machine power began to replace human, and animal, power throughout much of the world. It was a time of great change that affected people's way of life. During the Industrial Revolution, products were mass-produced for the first time. Factories were built. Cities grew. People began working at jobs that had never existed before.

The Industrial Revolution made just about everything in modern life possible. Without it, there would be no automobiles or airplanes. No electricity or electronics. No telegraph or telephones. No computers or the internet. No cell phones or social media.

Historians all agree that the success of the

Industrial Revolution came at a cost.

Because of the Industrial Revolution, weapons are now deadlier. Cities are much more crowded. And the environment has suffered greatly.

Historians also agree that the Industrial Revolution began near the middle of the eighteenth century. After that, they don't agree on much. Some believe that it lasted through the early 1900s. Some believe the Industrial Revolution went on for about a hundred years or

so, paused for a while, then picked up again in the early twentieth century. Others believe that there have been several industrial revolutions. (They say we are in the Fourth Industrial Revolution right now.) And still others believe that the Industrial Revolution never really ended. They say the "revolution" really has just been one long "evolution."

Everyone agrees, though, that the Industrial Revolution changed the world forever.

CHAPTER 1
Before the Industrial Revolution

The Industrial Revolution began in Great Britain in the mid-1700s. But its roots go back even farther than that.

Before then, people in Britain mostly stayed close to home. More than three out of every four workers farmed the land. Others worked in small workshops, making items such as shoes, furniture,

and especially, clothing. Most of the food that people ate they grew themselves. The things they used they made themselves. If not, they were grown or made by someone close by in their own community.

But Britain's population was increasing rapidly in the eighteenth century. In 1700, about 6.5 million people lived in England, Wales, and Scotland. That figure grew to 7.9 million in 1750. By 1800, it was almost 11 million! Those people had to be fed and clothed. Old ways of doing things needed to be improved to meet new needs.

Why Did the Industrial Revolution Start in Britain?

"Britain" is a shorter name for Great Britain, an island off the coast of continental Europe. It includes the countries of England, Scotland, and Wales.

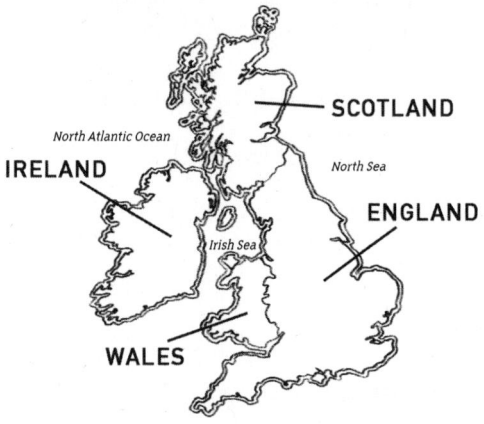

United Kingdom of Great Britain and Ireland during the Industrial Revolution

England stood as the most powerful nation on earth at the start of the Industrial Revolution. One big reason for this was its dominance of the seas. Because of Great Britain's geography, England featured many ports, which helped it maintain a vast navy of strong and fast ships. That navy helped it to conquer faraway lands and form the massive British Empire, with colonies around the globe. In the colonies, people in foreign countries lived under British rule, which offered them some of the security and stability of the British government. But it also forced them to live in obedience to outside rule, sometimes in very harsh conditions. And their natural resources and raw materials—which included anything from their crops to their gold—now belonged to their British colonizers. These raw materials, such as cotton from India, helped make England the world's richest country.

Those geographical and wealth advantages helped Britain take the lead in launching the Industrial Revolution.

One way to feed the growing population was to use better farming methods. Helpful tools such as steel plows and hoes were stronger and lasted longer than the older wooden ones. New methods of rotating crops kept the soil rich, yielding more vegetables. New ideas about breeding livestock led to better and more plentiful meat. Such improvements contributed to the cycle of population growth. The more and healthier food that people ate, the longer they lived. And the longer they lived, the more the population grew.

More people and more food meant that ways of cooking were changing, too. Coal had been around for thousands of years, of course. But until the sixteenth century, wood was cheaper and easier for British people to use for cooking and heating. Wood didn't burn as hot or last as long as coal. But coal emitted harmful fumes, and British houses were not built in a way that those fumes could safely escape. However, with the population growing so rapidly, demand for wood became greater than its supply by the seventeenth century. Wood became harder to come by and more costly. People needed an alternative—and England had a lot of coal.

By the start of the 1700s, coal had become Britain's primary fuel source. The faster and more efficiently that coal could be taken from the ground, the better and cheaper it would be for the people of Britain. Many scientists and engineers experimented with improved methods of mining coal. The most famous of these was a primitive steam engine designed by Thomas Newcomen in 1712. His machine burned coal to heat water. The resulting steam provided the energy to move a large piston up and down. Cold water cooled the

Thomas Newcomen

piston, then the process started all over again. This helped pump water out of mines and speed up the process for extracting coal. But the machine was also bulky and tall—more than thirty feet high—and wasted a lot of energy.

In addition, getting coal out of the ground was just half the battle. Coal was only found in

specific areas and still had to be transported to the people who needed it. Britain's port cities were well equipped for shipping. Many of its inland rivers were large enough for boats to use, too. And where it was not practical to use the sea or rivers, canals were built to move the coal by waterways. Overland, wagons or rail cars pulled by horses transported coal.

Clothing the increasing population was also

a challenge. The many people who made their own clothes often worked in cottage industries. Literally, these were people who made clothes by hand, at home in their cottages. But this was a slow process. Only one person at a time could operate a spinning wheel, which turned wool or cotton into yarn wrapped around a spindle (a revolving rod used to twist the yarn or thread). A loom, which weaved that yarn into cloth, required two people seated next to each other to operate it.

British inventor John Kay figured there must be a better way. In 1733, Kay invented the flying shuttle. This pulley system allowed one weaver to do the work previously done by two, and to do it faster. Then a big breakthrough came in 1764 when James Hargreaves, a weaver who lived near the town of Blackburn, England, designed the spinning jenny.

The idea for the spinning jenny came to Hargreaves when a spinning wheel tipped over. He noticed that the wheel kept on spinning, turning the spindle, even though it was upright. Why not put several spindles upright and close together? he wondered. He built a crude machine, and it worked! The new machine enabled a single spinner to produce yarn by working eight spools of thread at once.

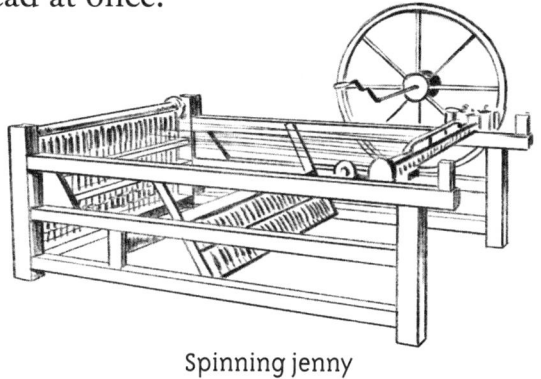

Spinning jenny

CHAPTER 2
The Birth of the Factory

The spinning jenny is often considered the invention that began the Industrial Revolution. It still took human hands to power, but it was the first big step toward automating the process of making clothes. It was the beginning of a new way of life. However, not everyone was on board with that new way of life.

James Hargreaves

James Hargreaves was a weaver himself, and he knew what his invention meant for spinners. It meant one spinner could do the work of eight. Many spinners wouldn't be happy about that. So he tried to keep his invention a secret. At first he used it only for his own work. But the community was a small one. Soon his close friends knew about it. Then rumors spread among fellow workers in the area.

As Hargreaves feared, they started to complain. The spinners thought the new machine would put them out of work. They wouldn't be able to provide for their families. The rumblings grew until, one day in 1768, a mob broke into Hargreaves's house. The angry spinners destroyed his invention.

Of course, Hargreaves could just build another spinning jenny. So he did just that. But not until he moved from his small town to the larger city of Nottingham, England—more than a hundred miles away.

In the end, the angry spinners were both right and wrong about their fears. Machines of the Industrial Revolution did indeed perform the work of many people. That meant fewer of certain kinds of jobs. So they were right about that. But they were wrong to think they wouldn't have any work. They didn't realize that more new jobs would be created. Many workers stopped doing the jobs they were used to in their own homes, but they did different or similar ones. This would happen again and again throughout the Industrial Revolution.

Later, members of the British Parliament rejected demands to ban the machines. They determined that the benefits of increased

production, quality, and efficiency outweighed the drawbacks. They were right. The changes increased demand, which increased the need for workers. For instance, more yarn being spun meant a greater need for weavers to turn that yarn into cloth. The big difference: Instead of working in their cottages or in small shops, they began working in factories.

One such factory was Richard Arkwright's cotton mill in Cromford, England. (A mill is a place where raw materials are converted into products, such as cotton into cloth, or wheat into flour.) Arkwright improved on the spinning jenny with a machine called the water frame—basically a spinning jenny powered by water instead of humans. It couldn't spin as many

Richard Arkwright

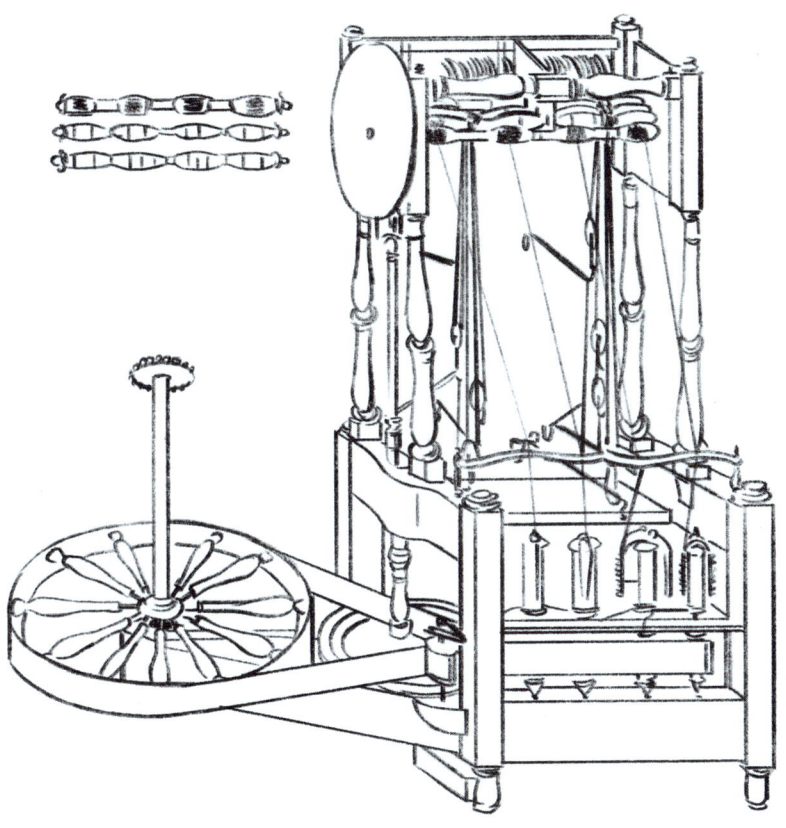

threads at one time as the spinning jenny, but it spun stronger yarn.

The water frame was a "clean" way of producing goods because it relied on a natural resource. (Burning coal and other fossil fuels is considered a "dirty" way of powering machines because it pollutes the air and can be harmful to the environment.) However, as its name suggests, Arkwright's invention needed a water source to power it. He found that source in 1771 in Cromford, where he built a five-story factory next to the River Derwent. Arkwright built water wheels in a nearby stream. Water from the current spun those wheels, which were connected to the machines inside. It was the first cotton spinning mill powered by water.

Cromford cotton mill

There were more jobs available in Arkwright's mill than men in Cromford available to fill them. So Arkwright built housing. He also hired many women and children—including some youngsters who were only seven!

At six o'clock in the morning, half of the workers checked in to the factory. The iron gates slammed shut behind them. If they were late, they didn't get in—and they didn't get paid. At six o'clock in the evening, those workers went home and the other half arrived. The iron gates slammed shut behind them. In this way, the factory was open twenty-four hours a day, six days a week.

The Spinning Mule

James Hargreaves's spinning jenny was good for producing large amounts of yarn. Richard Arkwright's water frame was good for producing strong yarn. Naturally, it didn't take long for someone to make a hybrid that combined the best of both. In 1779, British inventor Samuel Crompton built the spinning mule. (A mule is the offspring of two animals: a male donkey and a female horse.) The spinning mule produced greater amounts of better yarn.

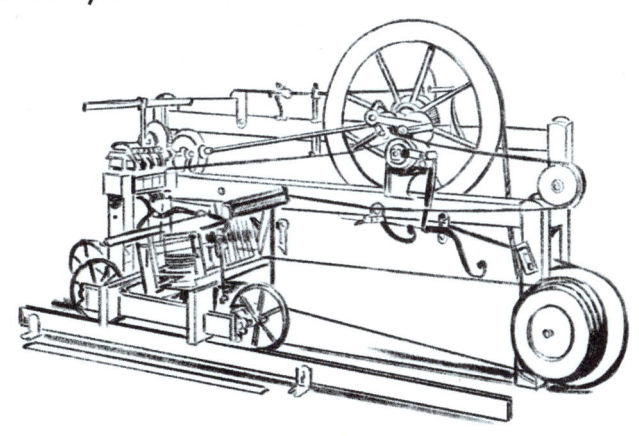

Arkwright became known as the "Father of the Factory System." His factory, and others like it, weren't perfect. Workers toiled for long hours. They were paid poorly. And the machines they worked on were incredibly noisy. But the new factories created many jobs. Factories like Cromford Mill, for instance, not only needed workers for the water frames but also others to build and repair the machines and the water wheels.

As with many developments in the Industrial Revolution, one new idea led to another. The building of factories led to better and cheaper products. Shoes, clothing, and tools that once had to be made slowly by hand were produced much faster. (They were less expensive because there were more products available.) That led to greater demand for those products. And that led to better technology for meeting demand.

Arkwright had harnessed the power of water

with the Cromford Mill. But no technology would prove more important than that which harnessed the power of steam.

CHAPTER 3
Full Steam Ahead

James Watt was an engineer at the University of Glasgow in Scotland when he was asked in 1764 to repair a steam engine of the kind built by Thomas Newcomen. He immediately saw how inefficient Newcomen's design was. Too much steam was wasted. Instead of fully powering the engine, some of it escaped. So Watt began working on his own design. After several years of tinkering, he built a new steam engine. And in 1769, Watt patented his ideas. In 1776, he and his business partner, Matthew Boulton, began selling the engine to manufacturers.

In Newcomen's engine, a single chamber was used for heating and cooling, driving a piston slowly up and down. Watt's steam engine was

James Watt and Matthew Boulton

different because he included a separate condenser chamber for the steam. Efficiency doubled, so the engine could be built smaller and use less coal. That meant it was less expensive to build and less expensive to use.

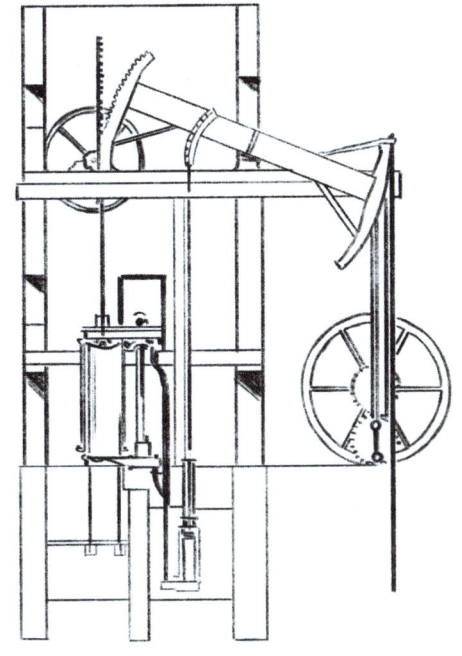

The Watt engine

In 1781, Watt added a "sun-and-planet" mechanism to his steam engine: One cogwheel (the "planet") was connected to a rod. Its teeth interlocked with another cogwheel (the "sun") that it revolved around. The sun-and-planet mechanism converted the up-and-down motion of the piston to a circular motion. That meant the steam engine had wide application. It could now be used on any number of machines that required circular motion. That made Watt's steam engine perhaps the single most important development of the Industrial Revolution. While Watt's design has always been modified for different uses, the fundamentals remain the same: water and heat generate steam, which generates power.

In 1785, Edmund Cartwright thought to use machine power instead of hand power to work a loom. (A loom holds threads in place so they can be woven into cloth.) Cartwright connected a steam engine to a system of gears and pulleys. Thus, the power loom was born. This sped up cloth production by automating the weaving process. In 1789, another of Cartwright's inventions automated combing wool. (Combing is a method of blending and arranging fiber for better texture and durability.) Cartwright's wool-combing machine reportedly could do the work of twenty people who combed by hand.

Edmund Cartwright

These many advances in technology had taken hold in Great Britain. But across the Atlantic Ocean, the United States would soon catch up.

A man who had worked for one of Arkwright's partners in England was Samuel Slater. He

moved to the United States in 1789, after the Revolutionary War had ended. At that time, the United States was still a very young country, having gained its independence from Great Britain in 1776.

While in Britain, Slater had learned a great deal about steam power and new methods of weaving cotton. And in 1793, in Pawtucket, Rhode Island, he opened the first successful cotton mill in the United States. He went on to

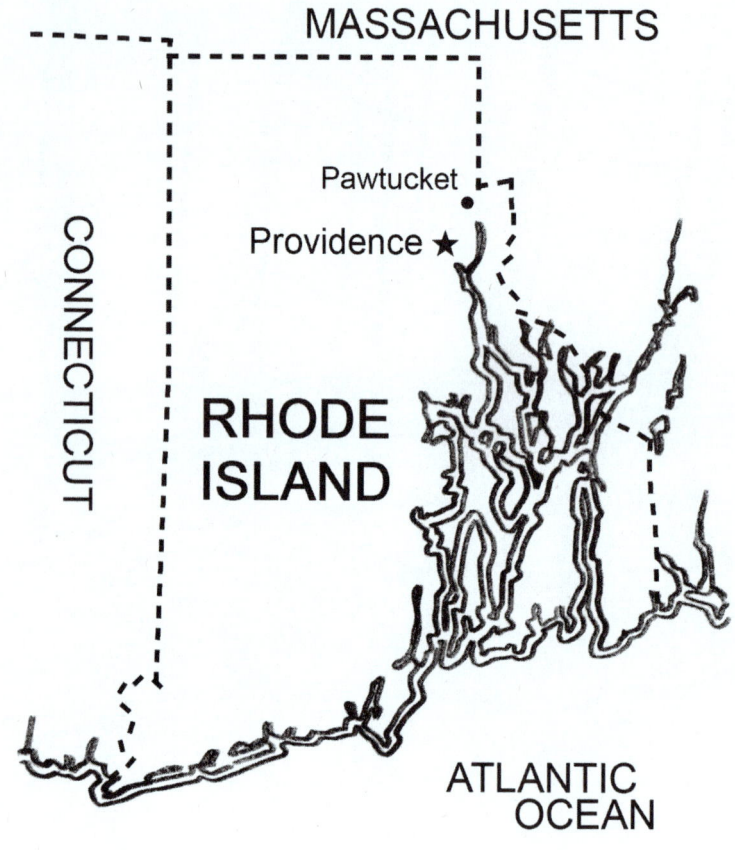

open several other mills in the New England area after that.

Andrew Jackson, who served as the seventh president of the United States from 1829 to 1837, would call Slater the "Father of the American Industrial Revolution." His nickname in his home country was not as nice. Some people, upset that he shared what he learned in Britain with people in the United States of America, called him "Slater the Traitor."

While the British-born Slater was the man who brought the Industrial Revolution to the United States, the biggest contribution was made by American-born inventor and engineer Eli Whitney. In 1793, Whitney built a mechanical cotton gin. (The name "gin" came from the word *engine*.)

Whitney's invention was not complicated, but it had a huge impact. After cotton was picked from plants, the soft fiber had to be separated from the seeds before it could be used to make clothing. The cotton gin simply was a way of doing that. And it could separate fiber ten times faster than by hand.

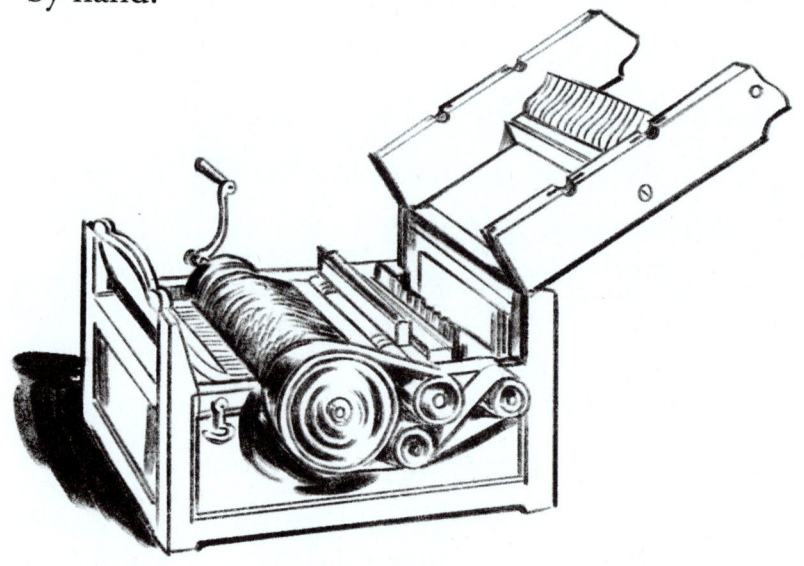

The cotton gin

Like many developments in the Industrial Revolution, the cotton gin was a mixed blessing. It was certainly a boon to the US economy, especially in the South. But it also contributed significantly to a rise in slavery.

The practice of enslaving people from the African continent had existed since 1619 in the colonies that later became the United States. But some historians have suggested that it might have ended sooner if not for Whitney's invention. It cost so much to buy, ship, and house enslaved people that many enslavers felt they were not

making enough money from their crops.

But with the cotton gin, US cotton production exploded. In 1793, the country produced about five million pounds. In 1800, it grew to thirty-five million pounds. Then, in 1807, the United States produced an astounding eighty million pounds.

All that cotton was picked by enslaved people who were owned by enslavers in the South. The slave system was now more profitable.

Enslaved people were a key part of three-way trade among the United States, Great Britain, and Africa. Enslaved people picked the cotton in the United States. Much of the cotton was then sent to Britain for manufacturing. In turn, Britain exported clothes, guns, and other factory products to countries in Africa that captured people for the United States to enslave.

Slavery lasted in the United States until the Thirteenth Amendment was ratified in 1865, shortly after the end of the Civil War.

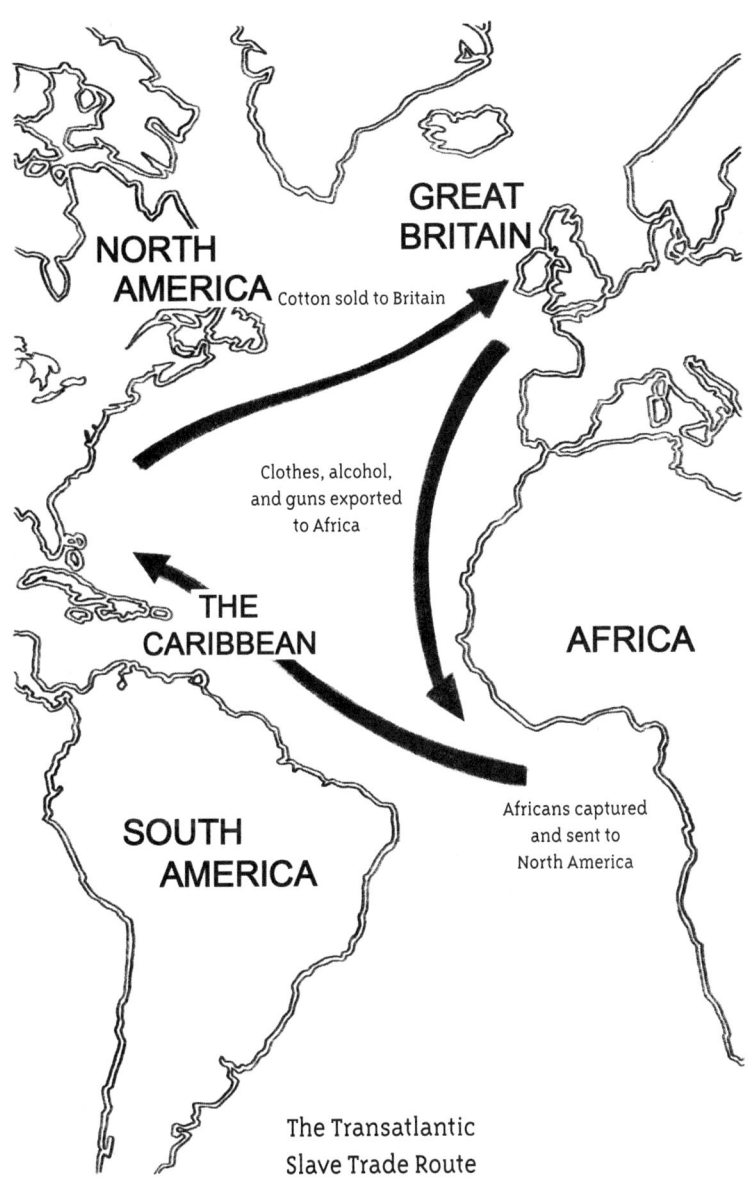

NORTH AMERICA

Cotton sold to Britain

GREAT BRITAIN

Clothes, alcohol, and guns exported to Africa

THE CARIBBEAN

AFRICA

Africans captured and sent to North America

SOUTH AMERICA

The Transatlantic Slave Trade Route

Eli Whitney (1765–1825)

Eli Whitney was born in what is now Massachusetts in 1765 and graduated from Yale College (now Yale University) in 1792. He was on his way to South Carolina to become a tutor when he detoured to Georgia and moved to a cotton plantation.

Eli Whitney

In 1798, Whitney agreed to produce ten thousand muskets (a type of gun) for the United States government in only two years. That was unheard of at the time because muskets were made by individual craftsmen one at a time. When they broke, they were not easily fixed. But Whitney proposed making identical individual parts that could fit any musket of the same design. He famously demonstrated his system in Washington, DC, to government officials, including President John Adams and President-Elect Thomas Jefferson.

Whitney ran into many supply problems and took ten years to produce the muskets he had promised in two. In the end, though, the government benefited from a high-quality product made at a lower cost. And Whitney helped popularize the idea of interchangeable parts.

CHAPTER 4
Railways

While the Industrial Revolution was advancing in the United States, further progress was happening in Great Britain, too.

On Christmas Eve in 1801, British mining engineer Richard Trevithick decided to take several of his friends out for a ride in the town of Camborne, England. But this was no horse-

Richard Trevithick

and-buggy ride. Trevithick's friends were going for the first drive in an invention of his. It was a steam engine attached to a wheeled carriage that was meant to be used on a road. Trevithick called it the Puffing Devil.

Spinning jenny, invented in 1764

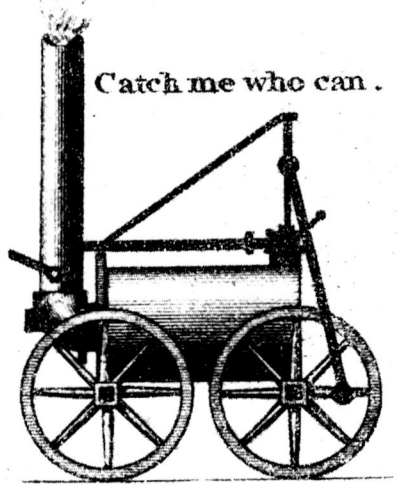

Ticket for Richard Trevithick's Catch Me Who Can locomotive, 1808

James Watt, inventor of the Watt engine

Richard Trevithick, inventor of the high-pressure steam engine

Painting of the race between the Tom Thumb locomotive and a horse in Baltimore, Maryland, by H. D. Stitt, 1830

Water wheel built in 1854 in the United Kingdom

Alexander Graham Bell making the first phone call
from New York to Chicago, 1892

The first Ferris wheel presented at the
Chicago World's Columbian Exposition, 1893

Cotton gin at the Dahomey Plantation in Mississippi, 1899

Women using power looms at a textile mill in Scotland,
early twentieth century

The Triangle shirtwaist factory fire in New York City, 1911

Ford Motor Company factory assembly line, 1913

Child factory workers at a spinning mill, early twentieth century

Steel factory workers striking in Chicago, 1919

Steam locomotive at the National Railway Museum in York, England, 1927

Factory pollution in Sheffield, England, 1927

The Puffing Devil chugged along the rough roads of Camborne, even pulling several people aboard up a hill. The passengers were amazed. It moved "faster than I could walk," one of them said.

Unfortunately, that was one of the few times the Puffing Devil took to the road. That's because the steam engine overheated on a drive several days later. Trevithick and his crew hopped off and went for a bite to eat and something to drink while it cooled down. While they were away, the Puffing Devil caught fire and was destroyed.

Trevithick was not deterred by the loss of the Puffing Devil, though. He didn't give up easily. He went back to his workshop and continued to tinker. One year later, Trevithick patented a high-pressure steam engine.

One constant in the Industrial Revolution is that any new invention was built on the knowledge and expertise of others and the ideas that came before it, even if just one person received the credit. Trevithick's high-pressure steam engine couldn't have happened without the major advances of James Watt.

Watt designed his engines to run on steam that produced low pressure. He scoffed at Trevithick's

idea of using higher pressure, believing the risk of explosion to be too dangerous. But advances in iron production enabled Trevithick to build a smaller, sturdier, and more powerful engine. It could withstand steam more than a dozen times the pressure of Watt's. Trevithick's boiler vented steam from the burning coal into the air. The sound of steam escaping gave the Puffing Devil its name.

Trevithick's Puffing Devil was built for the road. However, it was on the railways (called railroads in the United States) that his high-pressure engine had its biggest impact.

Earlier railway systems were made of wood and usually were no more than a few miles long. In the late eighteenth century, cast iron began to replace wood. Carriages on the cast-iron railways were still pulled by horses. But with iron wheels smoothly gliding along iron tracks, a single horse could pull about eight tons of coal.

In 1804, Trevithick mounted his steam engine on a trolley in Wales. The idea worked, but—as with the Puffing Devil—only for a short time. The weight of the engine was too great for the cast-iron rails, which broke. Nevertheless, Trevithick

had built the first working railway locomotive. It was a major moment in the Industrial Revolution. Steam locomotives would have far-reaching effects on manufacturing and transportation.

Catch Me Who Can

At first, railways were seen as a method for moving materials, such as coal, from place to place. But people—not so much.

Enough people were curious about the new steam locomotives, however, that Richard Trevithick found a way to make some money from the idea. In 1808, he built a locomotive to run on a track in London. He named it Catch Me Who Can.

Today, Catch Me Who Can would be considered a simple amusement park ride. It went around and around in a small circle. To keep the public curious, Trevithick surrounded it with a wall so it couldn't be seen from the outside.

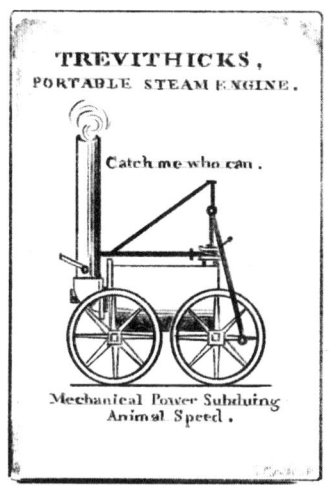

He charged an admission fee of two shillings (about eight US dollars today).

The circular track had a radius of about a hundred feet. (Radius is the measure from the center of a circle to its outer point.) But after the train started to run off the rails, Trevithick shut down the ride.

George Stephenson was a mine worker in England and the son of a steam engine fireman (the person who shoveled coal into a boiler to keep the fire going). In 1813, Stephenson engineered his version of a steam locomotive. Like Trevithick, he also ran into the problem of broken cast-iron rails. But iron makers soon produced wrought iron, which was stronger than cast iron, to make rails. And in 1825, Stephenson and his son, Robert, launched the era of the modern railway when they opened a track that stretched twenty-five miles between the collieries of Stockton and

George Stephenson   George's son, Robert Stephenson

Darlington. (A colliery includes a coal mine and its buildings and equipment.)

At first, Stephenson's railway mostly transported coal. And when the local price of coal almost immediately dropped because of the increased speed and efficiency of transport, American businesses took notice. Eventually, the idea of moving people caught on as well.

On Independence Day in 1828, construction began in the United States on the Baltimore and Ohio Railroad. Two years later, the Tom Thumb became the first American-built steam locomotive and had its famous race against a horse.

CHAPTER 5
Unintended Consequences

The Industrial Revolution produced an amazing number of useful inventions in the late eighteenth and early nineteenth centuries.

Each innovation propelled other technological shifts forward. But each also was met with some opposition. There were always people who didn't think machines were such a great idea. Some

thought a spinning mule, power loom, wool-combing machine, or others that followed would put them out of work. They believed it didn't take as much skill to operate the new machines as it did to make things by hand. And they felt that mill owners were getting rich while paying unfair low wages.

On the day of March 11, 1811, British troops were called in to break up worker protests in Nottingham. Then, that night, angry workers broke into a mill there and smashed its power looms to pieces. The protesters called themselves Luddites after Ned Ludd, a weaver who supposedly destroyed equipment in a mill more than thirty years earlier.

The Luddites

The Luddite disruption in Nottingham in 1811 led to many more such incidents in nearby towns in England over the next several months. Many factories had to be protected by soldiers, others by guards hired by mill owners. In some cases, demonstrations turned bloody. Protesters, and even mill owners, were killed. Some of the worst incidents came in the spring of 1812.

By 1813, the Luddite movement faded away. Some protesters were convicted of crimes. Others began to realize the Industrial Revolution was creating more jobs than it was taking away. However, the name of the movement endured. To this day, people who are not in favor of modern technology are called Luddites.

Because the mills and factories sprung up in more urban areas, cities were where the work was. And cities were growing too fast. They became overcrowded. Manchester, England, for instance, had a population of seventy-five thousand as the 1800s began. Thirty years later, it was nearly double that number. Sanitation was poor and drinking water unhealthy. But it would

Early sewage system in Manchester

be Industrial Revolution technology that helped solve the Industrial Revolution–created problems. For instance, new sewage systems were designed to keep waste out of rivers and streams. They helped to make water safe to drink again.

Businesses were so successful in Manchester that by the mid-1800s, more than one hundred cotton mills operated there. In 1830, George and Robert Stephenson built a railway linking Manchester with the port city of Liverpool, thirty-five miles away. It was the first railway in the world between two cities. Raw cotton, much of it coming from the United States, arrived in Liverpool, then was transported to Manchester. Eventually, almost one-third of all cotton fabric in the world was manufactured in Manchester. It became nicknamed "Cottonopolis." Business thrived in Cottonopolis. But so did pollution. The air became thick and grimy with smoke from burning coal. The environment was so polluted,

the sun had difficulty shining through the haze.
The city was noisy from all the machines operating
day and night.

The cotton mills relied heavily on child workers. Some were as young as seven or eight. For mill owners, there were several benefits. For one, they didn't pay children very much. For another, children had the energy to work long hours. And they were small enough to squeeze into places under and behind equipment to make repairs or to fix broken threads.

Of course, this wasn't good for the children. They were spending their days in the factory instead of in school. They were making very little money. And they were doing dangerous work. There were many incidents of children getting caught in the machinery.

Not all mill owners took unfair advantage of children. Some limited their hours. Others built schools on their property and hired tutors to help with education. But there was enough abuse that a movement grew to improve working conditions for children.

The Factory Act of 1833

Parliament passed laws in 1802 and 1819 to restrict child labor. But these had little effect because they were not enforced. It wasn't until 1833 that a system for inspection and penalties was established. The Factory Act of 1833 did not allow workers to be younger than nine years old, and limited the working hours to eight for those aged nine to twelve. It also required mill owners to provide two hours of schooling each day for anyone younger than thirteen.

CHAPTER 6
Great Inventions

Few people had seen a steam-powered printing press that could run off ten thousand pages an hour. Nor a machine that could fold envelopes by itself. Nor a voting machine. But visitors to the Great Exhibition in London in 1851 saw all those things and more—much more. "Every conceivable invention!" Britain's Queen Victoria wrote in her diary. She attended the exhibition thirty-four times!

Officially, the show had the clunky title of the Great Exhibition of the Works of Industry of All Nations. Unofficially, it was the first modern world's fair. It gave Britain a chance to show the world its many recent inventions. It also gave other countries of the world a chance to show

Queen Victoria at the
Great Exhibition

Britain that they were taking part in the Industrial Revolution, too.

The exhibition featured fifteen thousand exhibitors displaying more than one hundred thousand items. Some were simply objects of curiosity, but many others were modern machines—or products made possible by those machines.

Dozens of countries from around the world participated in the Great Exhibition, which was held at the Crystal Palace in London's Hyde Park.

The Crystal Palace

From the United States, there was a mechanical reaper (a machine used to harvest crops). From India, a variety of beautiful woven cloth and fabric. From Canada, a modern fire engine. Several countries exhibited their version of a sewing machine.

The Great Exhibition showed how quickly the Industrial Revolution was changing the world. And the years after the exhibition produced many more innovations on both water and land.

On the water, improved steam power and ironmaking were put into ship construction during the American Civil War. Also known as the Battle of Hampton Roads, the Battle of the *Monitor* and *Merrimack* did not have an impact on the outcome of the war. However, it marked a major turning point in the history of naval

warfare because it was the first time two ironclad ships fought each other.

During nearly four hours of head-to-head combat in 1862, neither the *Monitor* nor the *Merrimack* was able to gain an advantage. Then both ships returned to their respective homes. The fight was a draw, but navies around the world,

including those of powerful Britain and France, took notice that neither ship suffered significant damage. They realized that the future was in iron ships, and they stopped making vessels with wooden hulls.

On land, construction began in 1863 on the transcontinental railroad—a continuous rail line

that connected existing lines in the eastern United States with the rapidly expanding population on the West Coast. The US government provided the land; the Central Pacific and Union Pacific railroads took on most of the construction. And on May 10, 1869, the last spike in the transcontinental railroad was driven into the ground. That opened economic opportunities throughout the United States. Raw materials and products could now be moved more easily and cheaply from coast to coast—and everywhere in between.

Men such as John D. Rockefeller and Cornelius Vanderbilt amassed enormous personal fortunes in oil, railroads, and shipping, while building business empires. Sometimes, they were called "robber barons." That wasn't a nice term! It was because some people felt they got rich by being dishonest or taking advantage of other people, and that they paid unskilled workers unfairly low

John D. Rockefeller

Cornelius Vanderbilt

wages. These workers, many of them immigrants, built railroads and office buildings, and worked in factories. One of the most famous robber barons was Andrew Carnegie. He started the company that became the largest part of US Steel.

Steel is processed from the elements iron and carbon. It is a stronger metal than iron. Improved methods for producing steel made possible the skyscrapers, bridges, and ships of the Industrial Revolution.

Andrew Carnegie (1835–1919)

Andrew Carnegie was born in Scotland in 1835 but moved to the United States with his family when he was twelve. He and his business partners bought several steel mills in the Pittsburgh area, which they eventually merged to form Carnegie Steel in 1892. Nine  years later, Carnegie Steel joined with Federal Steel Company, National Steel Company, and several smaller companies to become US Steel.

That deal made Carnegie one of the richest people in America, and he spent the rest of his life helping others. He funded more than 2,500 libraries in the United States and Great Britain. He also funded schools, including Carnegie Mellon University in Pittsburgh, with his vast fortune.

In 1876, the United States hosted its own world's fair. The Centennial Exhibition was held in Philadelphia in the one-hundredth anniversary year of the founding of the United States.

Industrial Revolution inventions at the exhibition included Alexander Graham Bell's telephone, a steam-powered elevator, and an early

Alexander Graham Bell and his telephone

internal combustion engine (the kind of engine that would eventually power cars). Most notably, a seven-hundred-ton steam engine generated all the energy needed for the 558,440-square-foot Machinery Hall.

Three years later, Thomas Edison made the first practical incandescent lightbulb. Some say the lightbulb kept the Industrial Revolution going. Others say it launched a whole new Industrial Revolution, often called the Second Industrial Revolution. Much of the Second Industrial Revolution overlapped with the first. But during the Second Industrial Revolution, the focus of manufacturing and invention shifted to the United States.

Thomas Edison (1847–1931)

Thomas Alva Edison was an American businessman whose inventions helped shape the Second Industrial Revolution. He is most famous for the lightbulb and the phonograph, but he also invented hundreds of other products in his lifetime. He improved on the inventions of other people, too, such as the motion-picture camera, typewriter, and rechargeable battery. A tireless worker, Edison was nicknamed the "Wizard of Menlo Park" after the town in New Jersey where his laboratory was located.

In 1893, the World's Columbian Exposition in Chicago showcased the United States' growing role in the Industrial Revolution. More than twenty-five million people visited the fair in the six months it was open from May through October. Many of them were dropped off and picked up at a twenty-six-track train station built just for the fair. Once there, they could ride the first Ferris wheel or a moving sidewalk along the lakefront.

They marveled at an automatic dishwasher and tried out a new convenience in clothing called the zipper. But the real star of the show might have been the lighting: Nearly two hundred thousand lightbulbs shone at the first all-electric fair ever.

CHAPTER 7
Into the Twentieth Century

In the early 1900s, it took a long time to build a car. A group of workers at the Ford Motor Company needed about twelve hours to complete just a chassis (the body of a car) for the earliest Model T cars in 1908. Mass production was one of the hallmarks of the Industrial Revolution, but it was not yet widespread in the automobile industry. Cars generally were still made one at a time.

Then one day, an engineer at Ford had an idea. What if car makers copied the process used by other industries? Some meat packers used a trolley system to move the meat along as it was disassembled. Why not move a chassis a similar way to assemble a car?

Henry Ford, the founder of the company, knew it was a good idea. He began experimenting with different ways to make an assembly line work. He hired a motion-study expert. He broke the process into eighty-four steps. And he trained workers to perform specific individual tasks.

Henry Ford

Ford's moving assembly line debuted in 1913. And the result was dramatic. The assembly line cut the time to make a car to just ninety-three minutes.

Ford did not invent the assembly line, but he brought it to the car-making business. He was the first to make mass-produced cars affordable for the general public.

Ford's assembly line increased production while cutting costs. He began selling more automobiles than all other car makers in the United States combined! Other businesses saw Ford's success and followed suit. The assembly line became one of the Industrial Revolution's most lasting effects.

Another of Ford's ideas was to pay his workers a better salary. In 1914, he doubled their pay. Later, he also cut the work week down to forty hours. These changes had two great benefits: They kept his workers from getting bored doing the same tasks over and over. And they allowed them to afford to buy the cars they were building.

Not all other businesses copied this part of Ford's success in the early 1900s. As more low-paid, unskilled workers began doing repetitive tasks once reserved for skilled craftsmen, the divide between management and employees grew. The rich (managers and owners) got richer. The poor (laborers) stayed poor. And workplace safety wasn't always a priority.

Improvements often came only after workers organized into labor unions and went on strike. That means they didn't show up for work until the bosses agreed to increase pay or improve safety or working conditions—or all of the above. But

only about 10 percent of the American workforce belonged to labor unions in the early 1900s. Change was not always easy to bring about.

Worse still, significant change sometimes only came after the heavy cost of workers' lives. In

1911, for instance, the Triangle shirtwaist factory fire in New York killed 146 workers (144 of them at the scene; two later died at a hospital from their injuries). It led to major reforms in workplace safety and fire codes. It also led to the growth of the International Ladies' Garment Workers' Union, which became one of the largest and most powerful workers' unions in the United States.

Triangle Shirtwaist Fire

Late in the afternoon on Saturday, March 25, 1911, a fire broke out on the eighth floor of the Asch Building in New York City. The Triangle Waist Company, which made shirtwaists (a type of women's blouse), occupied the upper three floors of the ten-story building. About five hundred employees worked shoulder-to-shoulder on the three floors.

The fire likely was started by a discarded cigarette, even though smoking was not allowed in the factory. It quickly spread. There were no fire sprinklers in the building. There was only one fire escape, and it collapsed from the weight of workers trying to flee. Others rushed to the doors, only to find them locked from the outside by factory owners who were afraid of theft. Some of the 146 victims jumped to their deaths out of windows to avoid being consumed by flames. Many of the dead were immigrant women who had emigrated from Europe. Some were as young as fourteen.

In the aftermath of the fire, hundreds of thousands of people took to the streets of the city to protest worker conditions. Public and union pressure led to new safety measures in New York City. They included fire codes in all factory buildings, and new child labor laws. They became a model for similar laws throughout the country.

A different kind of tragedy in 1914 led to the outbreak of war. In June of that year, Archduke Franz Ferdinand of Austria-Hungary was shot to death by a Bosnian Serb named Gavrilo Princip. One month later, Austria-Hungary declared war on Serbia. Then other European countries began to take sides. Germany joined Austria-Hungary. The United States entered the war in 1917 on the Serbian side, which also included Britain, France, and Russia, among others.

World War I featured automated weapons, motorized tanks, airplanes, and steel battleships. The result was more than sixteen million people killed over the four years of the war. It was another example of the negative effects of the Industrial Revolution. Weaponry was now more deadly.

World War I ended in 1918. But it did not turn out to be the "War to End All Wars" as it was called at the time. Only twenty-one years later, the world was at war again. Weapons in World War II

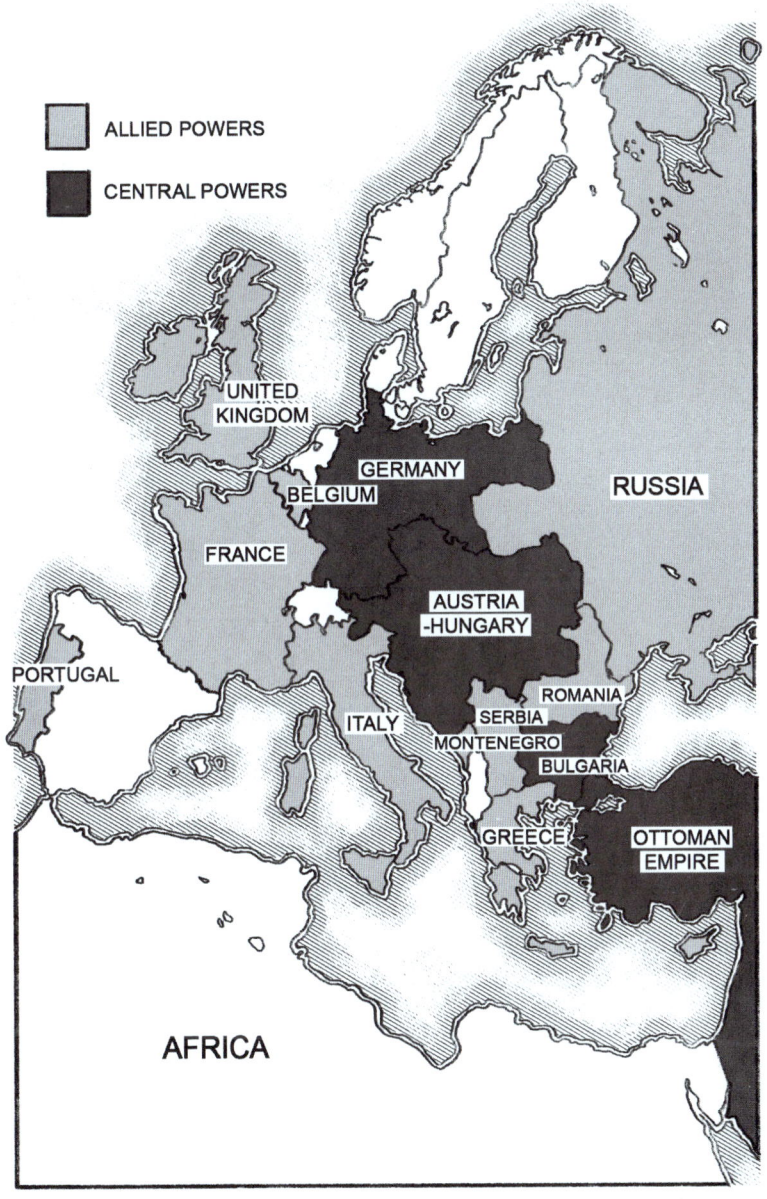

ALLIED POWERS

CENTRAL POWERS

UNITED
KINGDOM

GERMANY

BELGIUM

RUSSIA

FRANCE

AUSTRIA
-HUNGARY

PORTUGAL

ROMANIA

ITALY

SERBIA

MONTENEGRO

BULGARIA

GREECE

OTTOMAN
EMPIRE

AFRICA

were even more advanced, especially regarding air power. Planes were able to fly greater distances and drop more destructive bombs. The deadliest was the atom bomb, which the United States dropped on Hiroshima, Japan, on August 6, 1945. Three days later, a second atom bomb was dropped on Nagasaki, Japan.

The bombs quickly led to the end of the war.

But before the Industrial Revolution, people had not yet developed weapons to kill such a large number of people at one time. Now there were 120,000 dead in two blasts in Japan. (Thousands more also died later from the effects of the bombs.)

Once again, the Industrial Revolution had produced unwanted results.

CHAPTER 8
The Revolution Continues

Many history books close the Industrial Revolution, or the Second Industrial Revolution, around the time of the world wars in the first half of the twentieth century.

And yet, the story continues. It can be argued that the Industrial Revolution has never really ended. The invention of the transistor in 1947 ushered in another era of automated technology: the Digital Revolution, or the Third Industrial Revolution. The transistor continued the line

The transistor

of progress that began nearly two hundred years earlier with the spinning jenny.

Personal computer

The transistor was to the Third Industrial Revolution what water, coal, and steam were to the earliest days of the Industrial Revolution. And what the incandescent lightbulb and electricity were to the Second Industrial Revolution. It became the means for production in the computer and information age. This period from the middle of the twentieth century until early in the twenty-first gave us the personal computer, cell phones, and the internet. The transistor is what makes all those things—and many more—run.

Cell phone

Little Size, Big Role

Transistors are semiconductors (substances that can move either heat or electricity) in electronic devices. They are used for amplifying (making stronger) and controlling electrical signals.

Because of their amplification function, early transistors were useful for small radios and hearing

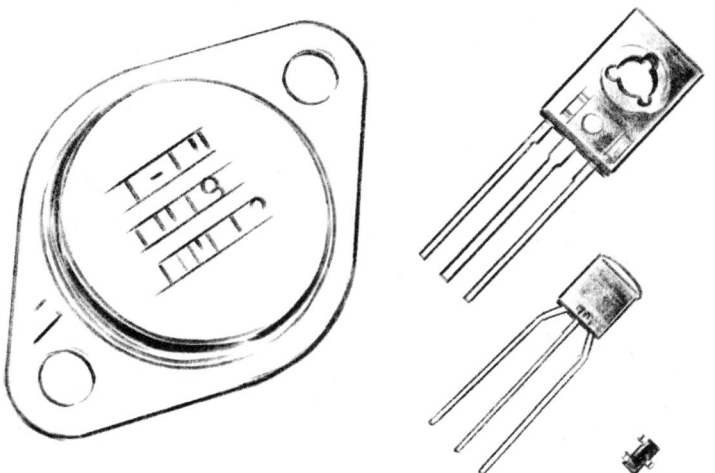

Modern transistor

aids. And because of their ability to allow or block the flow of electrical current, transistors became the primary building blocks for computers.

The earliest transistors were much smaller than the vacuum tubes they replaced—but much larger than they are now. In fact, the number of transistors on a microchip doubles every two years.

Transistors are so small that in 2023, the processor in an average smartphone had at least ten billion of them.

"Every once in a while, a revolutionary product comes along that changes everything," Apple chief executive Steve Jobs told an enthusiastic audience at his company's Macworld tech conference in San Francisco in 2007. Jobs was introducing the iPhone, Apple's version of a cell phone. The iPhone combined the benefits of a regular cell phone with the ability to use the internet, send messages via text, take photos, and listen to music. Other devices could do those things, but none combined them the way the iPhone did. The iPhone was the smartest smartphone built to date.

Steve Jobs and the iPhone

Business leaders often put the best possible spin on their claims in order to sell products. But in Jobs's case, he was right! By 2024, billions of people around the world owned smartphones. Estimates vary, but about one in every four of them was an iPhone.

The smartphone is so revolutionary that our current age is sometimes called the Fourth Industrial Revolution. It has brought us cloud computing, virtual reality, and the Internet of Things (everyday devices connected to a network, such as a home security system controlled from your phone).

It may seem strange to put a smartphone in the same category as a spinning jenny, but there is a clear link between the earliest days of the Industrial Revolution and the most modern technology. A line of progression can be drawn from the mid-eighteenth century to the artificial intelligence of today. Artificial intelligence, commonly called AI, refers to the ability of computer systems to perform tasks traditionally associated with human intelligence and to "learn" to problem solve.

The Rise of AI

Today, artificial intelligence and the Fourth Industrial Revolution are sparking many of the same concerns as past phases of the Industrial Revolution.

AI already is capable of performing many tasks previously done only by humans. It is the reason self-driving cars may be likely in the near future.

There is little doubt, then, that AI will replace many jobs. But will it create even more new ones? Will this phase of the Industrial Revolution be like those before it, changing our daily lives forever? Or will it come at too great a cost?

Because of the Industrial Revolution, the way we make things, the way we travel, and the way we communicate have completely changed. Today, we can't imagine a world without machines, cars, or the internet. But each new development in the Industrial Revolution creates new expectations. What once was considered new and exciting eventually seems old and slow. What will come next? Fourth Industrial Revolution advances such as self-driving vehicles and advanced robotics are closer than ever.

There is still a cost, of course. Global climate change disasters and cybersecurity (the tools needed to keep you safe when you are online) are just a couple of modern-age issues. Industrial Revolution technology helped cause these problems. It will likely take Industrial Revolution technology to solve them.

No one could have foreseen three hundred years ago that cutting-edge inventions such as the spinning jenny and the steam engine would lead to smartphones and artificial intelligence. But almost every facet of modern life can trace its origins to the Industrial Revolution.

Timeline of the Industrial Revolution

1712 — England's Thomas Newcomen builds the first practical steam engine for pumping water out of mines

1764 — James Hargreaves's spinning jenny marks the beginning of the Industrial Revolution

1771 — Cromford Mill, the first cotton-spinning mill powered by water, opens in England

1776 — Scottish engineer James Watt and business partner Matthew Boulton begin marketing their version of a more efficient steam engine

1793 — Eli Whitney invents the cotton gin

1804 — British mining engineer Richard Trevithick builds the first working railway locomotive

1830 — The Tom Thumb steam locomotive races a horse on the Baltimore and Ohio Railroad in Maryland

1851 — The Great Exhibition in London showcases many advances of the Industrial Revolution

1876 — Alexander Graham Bell invents the telephone

1879 — Thomas Edison creates the first practical incandescent lightbulb

1913 — Henry Ford brings the assembly line to the car-making industry

1947 — The invention of the transistor marks the beginning of the Digital, or Third Industrial, Revolution

2007 — Apple introduces the iPhone

Timeline of the World

1712 — Nine people are killed in the New York Slave Revolt of 1712

1776 — On July 4, the United States' Declaration of Independence is adopted in Philadelphia

1789 — The French Revolution begins

1837 — Queen Victoria begins her sixty-three-year reign over the United Kingdom of Great Britain and Ireland

1848 — The California Gold Rush begins

1861 — The Civil War begins in the United States

1865 — The Thirteenth Amendment abolishes slavery in the United States

1871 — Welsh journalist Henry Morton Stanley finds missing Scottish explorer David Livingstone in Ujiji, Africa

1903 — The Wright brothers successfully fly a plane at Kitty Hawk, North Carolina

1906 — A major earthquake strikes near San Francisco, California, destroying much of the city

1941 — The United States enters World War II after its naval base at Pearl Harbor, Hawaii, is attacked by Japan

1947 — Jackie Robinson of the Brooklyn Dodgers becomes the first Black player in the modern era of Major League Baseball

2007 — American media company Netflix launches its video streaming service

Bibliography

*Books for young readers

Allitt, Patrick N. *The Industrial Revolution*. The Great Courses.
　　Chantilly, VA: The Teaching Company, 2014. DVD.

*Burgan, Michael. *Who Was Henry Ford?* New York:
　　Penguin Workshop, 2014.

"The Industrial Revolution in the United States." Library of
　　Congress. Accessed February 11, 2025. https://www.loc.gov/
　　classroom-materials/industrial-revolution-in-the-united-
　　states/.

*Marcovitz, Hal. *The Industrial Revolution*. Understanding World
　　History. San Diego: ReferencePoint Press, 2014.

*McDaniel, Melissa. *The Industrial Revolution*. Cornerstones of
　　Freedom. New York: Children's Press, 2012.

Morris, Charles R. *The Dawn of Innovation: The First American
　　Industrial Revolution*. New York: PublicAffairs, 2012.

*Tabler, Judith. *Not So Fast, Tom Thumb: The Story of the Horse
　　Who Raced an American Steam Locomotive*. Manchester
　　Center, VT: DartFrog Plus, 2023.